The Truth About Vikings

The TRUTH ABOUT VIKINGS

Jonny Walker

Illustrated by
Nuno Alexandre Vieira

Collins

Contents

Chapter 1 Vikings or medieval Scandinavians? 6

Bonus: Map of the Vikings 20

Chapter 2 Life, death and belief.......... 22

Bonus: Loki's family portrait 36

Chapter 3 Myth-busting!................... 38

Bonus: Connecting to Bluetooth 52

Chapter 4 The world of the Vikings 54

Bonus: More about the Birka burial....... 70

Chapter 5 Medieval Scandinavians in Britain................................. 72

Bonus: Norse words in English 86

Chapter 6 How do we know?.............. 88

Bonus: A recent discovery................ 102

Glossary 104

About the author 106

About the illustrator...................... 108

Book chat 110

 CHAPTER 1
Vikings or medieval Scandinavians?

When you hear the word Vikings, what do you think of? Axe-wielding men with beards? Helmets with horns?

Well … the people who lived in Scandinavia in early **medieval** times were more than just **raiders** and invaders. It's a story of both men and women. It's a tale of survival, conflict, faith and adventure that takes us all over the world.

The *real* story of the Vikings is much more interesting than just roaring raiders!

The Viking Age began over 1,000 years ago. Some historians say it lasted from around 750 CE to 1,000 CE. But, in reality, it's not always possible to give a single date when a historical period started or finished. Vikings were real people, so their lives didn't start and stop on exact dates.

The region of Scandinavia includes Denmark, Sweden and Norway.

During the Viking Age, Scandinavian raiders, **traders** and farmers arrived in coastal towns and villages across Europe, sometimes using force, and sometimes by making deals with people already living there.

BCE/CE

In history, you'll often see these letters after a date. CE means 'Common Era', the time after the year 0. BCE means 'Before Common Era', before the year 0.

Some Vikings rowed long distances along rivers, going east as far as Russia. Some then sailed to the city now known as Istanbul. Some crossed the Atlantic Ocean to places we now know as Greenland and Canada!

But what does the word 'viking' actually mean? Confusingly, it means several different things.

Medieval Scandinavians spoke the Old Norse language.

In Old Norse, a *vikingr* was somebody who went on journeys overseas. Raiders and invaders were 'vikingrs', but so were traders and farmers who travelled to grow crops and tend animals in new lands.

A similar word, *vikingar*, had a different meaning. *Vikingar* was an insult, describing violent pirates who showed no mercy to those they raided. In fact, Scandinavian rulers often worked against the *vikingar*!

Today, Vikings can refer to all medieval Scandinavians, and blends both definitions.

The history of the word 'Viking' might explain their violent reputation today. It's pretty harsh that the word used to describe violent pirates became the word we use to describe all medieval Scandinavian people!

Some medieval Scandinavians enjoyed violent raids, bloodshed and fearless fury. These tended to be young adults, mostly men, who saw raiding as an exciting kind of 'get-rich-quick' scheme. In many ways, they were right. Those young Scandinavians who took to the seas often returned home weighed down with stolen silver, jewellery and confidence.

Recent archaeological evidence suggests there could have been some raiding women too.

But most people were too busy caring for their cabbages, worshipping their gods and feeding their geese!

Life in medieval Scandinavia was tough! Your survival depended on the health of your crops and your animals. If the crops did not grow, or if the animals became diseased, people would die. So, above all else, the medieval Scandinavians became skilful farmers.

Working the land was the main activity for everybody, children included. Sowing seeds, harvesting crops and tending to animals were all important parts of the job.

Dairy production, cloth-making and weaving were crucial too.

Daily life was exhausting, but hard times breed tough people. To be a farmer in medieval Scandinavia, you needed to be just as resilient and fearless as the raiders who travelled across seas to fight against unknown enemies.

Medieval Scandinavians lived in **longhouses**. These buildings were long – you probably guessed that – and contained different spaces. They were usually built onto wooden frames, with walls made of planks and logs. The floor was a sprinkling of dirt and ash. Medieval Scandinavians lit small fires indoors, for cooking, heating and light.

a reconstructed Viking longhouse in Fyrkat, Denmark

There was a hole in the roof for smoke to escape, but the constant fires ensured that smoke remained heavy in the air.

Archaeologists recently discovered that some longhouses had tiny decorative windows, but this was a rare luxury for the very wealthy.

> **FACT**
> Our word 'window' comes from Old Norse *windauga* meaning 'wind-eye'.

Life in a longhouse was lively, cramped and noisy with lots of different activities going on.

People lived, worked and slept in just one side of the longhouse. Here, textiles and cloth were spun on the loom. Food was cooked and eaten. Tools were carved, animal skins were dyed, and the blacksmiths forged axe-heads. Babies were nursed, children played board games.

Viking gaming

These 14 antler/bone game pieces were found in a Viking boy's grave in Scotland. Gaming looked a little different in around 850 CE.

Wealthier families may have had a bed for the master and mistress, but everybody else slept on wooden benches. There might have been up to 50 people sharing the space together, so let's just say the Vikings did not have much personal privacy!

Why not use the other half of the longhouse, if it was so cramped? Well, that was for the **livestock** during winter. In some ways, it was helpful having cattle, sheep, goats and horses heating the cold air with their warm bodies. But … just imagine the stench!

It would be wrong to conclude that the Vikings were perfectly calm people living a simple life in their longhouses, though. The medieval Scandinavians who did go across the seas to raid and attack deserved their fearsome reputation! Raiders grouped together, boarded their boats and crossed dangerous waters in search of anything worth taking.

The raiders were so feared by those they invaded that even now, over 1,000 years later, the common impression remains of Vikings as monstrous, bloodthirsty killers. Partly, this is because the main way we know about the Vikings is through the writings of their enemies.

From the perspective of their enemies, the invaders were wild, lawless and godless. At the beginning of the Viking Age, much of Western Europe had converted to Christianity. The Vikings who arrived in their lands were seen as 'heathens', meaning people who acted against Christianity.

Whilst the written accounts of the Vikings' enemies were extremely important and useful, helping us to understand what happened, it's fair to say they might have been biased.

The earliest writings from England about the Vikings told of 'heathen armies' destroying monasteries and attacking priests. These acts shocked the Christian communities of Europe, and news quickly spread about these 'godless **Norsemen**'.

But it wasn't true that the medieval Scandinavians were godless. They believed in what the Christians saw as the 'old gods', like Thor, Odin, Frigg and Freyr. The beliefs of the medieval Scandinavians remain well-known today, no longer as a living religion but in the tales of Norse mythology.

Bonus
Map of the Vikings

This map shows all the places that we know the Vikings visited. The Vikings settled in some of the places; others were raided or invaded.

CHAPTER 2
Life, death and belief

We consider stories about Norse gods to be myths. But for medieval Scandinavian people, these stories and gods were at the heart of their religious beliefs.

Their beliefs, known as Norse paganism, were shared among other groups of people who lived across Northern Germany and Scandinavia. In fact, they were shared by some **Anglo-Saxons** in Britain too!

The people of Southern Britain (because England didn't exist yet) were mostly Anglo-Saxon. Their ancestors came from Northern Europe.

Medieval Scandinavians had a complex network of gods and goddesses as well as a complex creation story.

They believed that the world was formed when Odin and his brothers Vili and Ve destroyed a frost giant named Ymir. The siblings made the world from the dead giant's body parts – Ymir's skin became earth, his head became the heavens and his blood became the sea.

The Aesir and the Vanir were two different 'families' of gods – sometimes at war, sometimes united.

The Aesir included gods like Odin, Thor and Hel.

Odin 'The Allfather' – god of wisdom, magic, war and death

Thor – god of thunder

Hel – goddess of death and decay

The Vanir included gods like Njordr, and his children Freyr and Freyja. Kvasir is often seen as part of the Vanir too, though he was created from the saliva of both families, as part of a peace pact!

Njordr – god of sea, wind and wealth

Freyr – god of fertility, peace and good weather

Freyja – goddess of love, beauty, war and magic

Kvasir – god of peace, extreme wisdom and the birth of poetry

The world of the medieval Scandinavians also included many creatures, beasts and beings, plenty of whom seem terrifying and/or unusual to modern eyes.

- Brunnmigi – meaning 'pees in a well'. An annoying troll that pollutes water sources.
- Hafgufa – An enormous sea monster that looks like an island with a mouth.
- Jormungandr – the colossal 'World Serpent' that encircles Earth.
- Huldra – a beautiful human-like forest creature with a cow tail that lures you to your doom.

Medieval Scandinavians believed that the world was divided into nine different realms. The land of the humans was called Midgard, but there were also lands of giants, lands of the gods and lands of the dead. The whole world is Yggdrasil (igg-drah-sil), the 'World Tree', whose trunk, roots and branches connect all the realms together.

Nothing is more important than Yggdrasil. When the World Tree dies, everything dies (even the gods). Therefore, the tree must be nurtured and protected.

The beliefs of the Norse people formed part of their everyday life. When Viking fighters charged into battle, it seemed they did not fear death. It was as if they welcomed it, in fact! Their belief in the afterlife might explain some of this faith.

Medieval Scandinavians believed that warriors who died bravely in battle were carried by '**Valkyries**' to Valhalla. Valhalla is the banqueting hall of Odin, the ultimate reward for those who faced death with a smile.

Some fighters were *so* empowered by their worship of Odin, that they flayed bears and wore their skins into battle! Imagine psyching yourself up to fight the invaders, when suddenly a blood-soaked axe-wielding bear comes charging at you!

These animal-wearing warriors were known as **berserkers** – *ber* meaning bear, and *serk* meaning shirt. Even today, we can describe somebody acting with the wildness of an animal as having 'gone berserk'.

For medieval Scandinavian people, your destiny was not in your own hands. Instead, the story of your life was decided by powerful beings called Norns.

Different sources describe Norns in different ways, the most important source is an Old Norse poem called *Völuspá*, which describes three Norns – Urd, Verdandi and Skuld. They represent the past, present and future.

The Norns were said to spend their time at the loom, where they weaved the fate of each human into the cloth of life. In some of the old stories, a Norn visits each newborn child and decides its future.

The Norns live in a great hall beside the Well of Fate, beneath the branches of the World Tree. They take water from the well, and water the roots, keeping Yggdrasil alive.

Not all medieval Scandinavians would have believed in the same stories, even when they believed in the same gods. Like the Greeks and Romans before them, the Vikings crossed many areas of the world, and different versions of their beliefs grew up in different places.

Norse beliefs can be found in our days of the week. Across many languages and cultures, the days of the week are named after gods. The French words for the days of the week are named after Roman gods:

Lundi	Mardi	Mercredi	Jeudi	Vendredi
Luna day	Mars day	Mercury day	Jupiter day	Venus day

The medieval Scandinavians had a very similar system with their own gods. These new names for the days of the week were used by the Anglo-Saxons and Vikings, who settled in Britain.

Monday	Tuesday	Wednesday	Thursday	Friday
Moon day	Tiw's/Tyr's day	Woden's/Odin's day	Thunor's/Thor's day	Frigg's day

It's clear that the medieval Scandinavians had knowledge of the Greek and Roman gods, and what they represented.

Tuesday's Norse god Tyr is a god of war, like Mars.

Wednesday's Odin and Mercury are both 'soul guides' taking mortals to the afterlife.

And Thursday's gods Thor and Jupiter are both thundering sky gods.

Sacrifice was part of daily life. It wasn't just about worshipping the gods, either – the medieval Scandinavians made offerings to nature spirits.

Archaeologists have found evidence of buildings designed purely for sacrificial ritual. These included narrow but tall chambers, with gold-foil figures in the walls, and a platform for sacrificing objects like gold and jewellery.

Sacrifice was often a messy business. Animals and even humans were sacrificed. These sacrifices may have been used like prayers, asking for safe travel, good fortune in battle, or for a healthy harvest.

Vikings also made bog sacrifices and water sacrifices, placing valuable weapons, metals, coins and jewellery into bogs and lakes as offerings to the unseen creatures below the surface.

This practice proved very helpful for archaeologists thousands of years later, as the wet conditions of the bogs preserved the objects.

Peat bogs contain very little oxygen, which means the bacteria that cause things to rot and decay can't survive. Therefore, bog-buried objects are often well-preserved.

Bonus
Loki's family portrait

The god Loki has four children who are ... unusual.

CHAPTER 3
Myth-busting!

For many years, the Vikings have been a major part of popular culture. Video games, TV shows, films and manga have all mined Norse myths and histories to tell exciting stories. Because of this, the true story of the Norse people, including those Viking raiders, can easily get lost.

Many things that people think are true are actually rumours, misunderstandings or artistic license!

It doesn't help that there's little written or archaeological evidence from the time of the Vikings.

Today, we can still read the words of many ancient Greek poets, study their buildings and examine their statues. We can learn about the Golden Age of Islam by looking at the journals of scholars and historians living in Baghdad.

This is much trickier when studying medieval Scandinavians, who didn't write much down.

So, let's do some myth-busting – smashing through the falsehoods to find the facts!

They had horns on their helmets!

The most famous **stereotype** of the Vikings is of bearded shouty men wearing horned helmets. The beard and shouting bit were often true, but not the horned helmet.

We can trace this to a costume designer called Carl Emil Doepler. When staging an opera featuring Vikings, he gave their helmets horns so they would stand out more.

There is no archaeological evidence that helmets with horns were part of the Viking wardrobe. The helmets that have been found look like this one from the south of Norway.

But to complicate things, a 1,200-year-old tapestry was discovered that *did* show a figure with a horned helmet. Perhaps this means horned helmets were used sometimes – maybe for ceremonies? Or the tapestry was showing a mythical figure?

All we know is it would be very difficult to fight with a whopping pair of horns stuck on your head, and there's no archaeological evidence of a helmet like this.

Who knows, though? Perhaps it is waiting to be discovered beneath the soil.

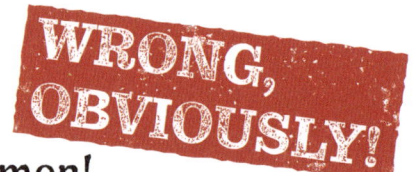

They were all men!

Most of what we know about medieval Scandinavians comes from the writings of people they invaded. Overwhelming evidence tells us that raiders were male – there is no conclusive archaeological evidence of female raiders, so perhaps that explains a little about why the history of the Vikings feels like a history of murderous men.

However, recent discoveries are changing our understanding of the role of women and girls in Norse society.

A remarkable burial site was excavated in Birka, Sweden, in 1878. Alongside the buried body, there were lots of different weapons as well as board games and two horses.

It was very clearly the grave of a powerful and important person. For many years, archaeologists had assumed that this weapon-rich grave must have belonged to a male warrior, perhaps even a commander.

However, in 2017, a study of the skeleton revealed that this person was female.

Perhaps this proves the existence of at least one prominent female warrior?

The graves of at least two other probable female warriors have been discovered in Norway, and future research may unearth more.

Vikings looked alike

Whenever we see representations of Vikings, they are almost always pale with red or blonde hair.

The Viking raiders travelled far and wide – across Europe, across the Atlantic Ocean, and even downriver towards West Asia. The majority of raiders were white Scandinavians from across what we know today as Denmark, Sweden and Norway.

But there is archaeological and genetic evidence that shows the Vikings themselves were much more mixed.

The raiding parties often picked up new members along the way – local people seizing the chance for a different life. In Viking-led settlements, such as Jorvik (modern-day York, England), life was very culturally and religiously diverse.

In 2020, a study of Viking burials in Scandinavia showed that several of the dead Vikings were not born in Scandinavia, but were from places like the British Isles, France and Eastern Europe.

Wherever the Vikings travelled, some people from those places joined them. Some went by choice and some were enslaved. This means that Vikings were not *exclusively* Scandinavian.

FACT
Not every Viking raider was born in Scandinavia!

They didn't write anything

It's true that medieval Scandinavians had low levels of literacy, and most people did not write. That was true of most places in medieval times! But this doesn't mean that Norse people had no written language at all.

Runes (and runic alphabets) were used by the Germanic people (which includes Scandinavians) from the 1st century. These runes were called Younger Futhark, named after the first six letters: f-u-þ-a-r-k.

þ is a letter that makes the 'th' sound, like in 'throne'

Younger Futhark contains 16 different runes.

Futhark runes were most often carved into hard surfaces like stone and wood. Some people say that runic alphabets contain no curved lines, but this is not true. Archaeological evidence of rune stones shows plenty of examples of wavy and curved lines.

The Karlevi rune stone, dating back to the late 10th century, features a poem about Thor's daughter, Thrud. It was found on a burial mound.

One interpretation of these words is that the dead leader buried in the mound might come back to life to seek revenge, with the assistance of Thrud. Thrud was the child of Thor and the goddess Sif – in some sources, she is considered to be a goddess of strength, and in others, a Valkyrie.

They were scruffy

The Vikings suffer from a bad reputation, and were often seen as being wild, unkempt and unclean, and that's not backed up by evidence.

Ibn Fadlan was a messenger from Baghdad, which was one of the most advanced empires in 922 CE. He and his fellow travellers were headed to meet the King of the Bulgars (the people Bulgaria is named after). To avoid danger, they took a very long route and because of this, they encountered many different people, including some Vikings.

As a scholarly person, Ibn Fadlan wrote about what he learned.

He saw Vikings' lack of toilet hygiene as very unclean, compared to the Islamic standards he was used to, but he also noted that they washed and combed their hair every day.

Meanwhile in Britain, the Vikings were seen as far cleaner and more attractive than the locals, who did very little bathing.

Thousands of handmade combs, tweezers and ear-picks, crafted from bone, have been found in archaeological digs across Scandinavia and wherever the Vikings visited. This matches the observations made by Ibn Fadlan.

It is worth adding that apart from their combing, Ibn Fadlan wrote that the Vikings were still 'the filthiest of God's creatures' because they all shared the same basin of water.

a selection of bone/antler combs discovered by archaeologists in Uppland, Sweden

Bonus

Connecting to Bluetooth

Meet Harald Bluetooth, King of Denmark

Harald Bluetooth united the tribes of Denmark into a single kingdom in the late 900s.

He is thought to have had a dead tooth, which would have been bluish in colour, hence the nickname.

He oversaw the creation of this famous rune stone, to celebrate his successes.

Bluetooth technology is named after him. The Bluetooth logo combines the Futhark runes H (ᚼ) and B (ᛒ).

CHAPTER 4
The world of the Vikings

Medieval Scandinavians did not live in isolation from the rest of the world – they raided and traded, which meant that Norse people were connected to other people across Europe and West Asia.

The medieval Scandinavians were skilful seafarers, experts at sailing across perilous seas. This skill (as well as their willingness to invade and fight) meant the Vikings went to many different parts of the world during the Viking Age.

The Vikings were not one army with a commander in charge. Each voyage brought together a mix of individuals from different regions, often united for that expedition alone. This meant their attacks could appear sudden and unpredictable, since there was no single plan – only small bands pursuing opportunity, wealth and adventure.

This incredibly well-preserved Viking ship was excavated from a burial mound in Norway. Inside it, archaeologists found two skeletons, both belonging to high-status women.

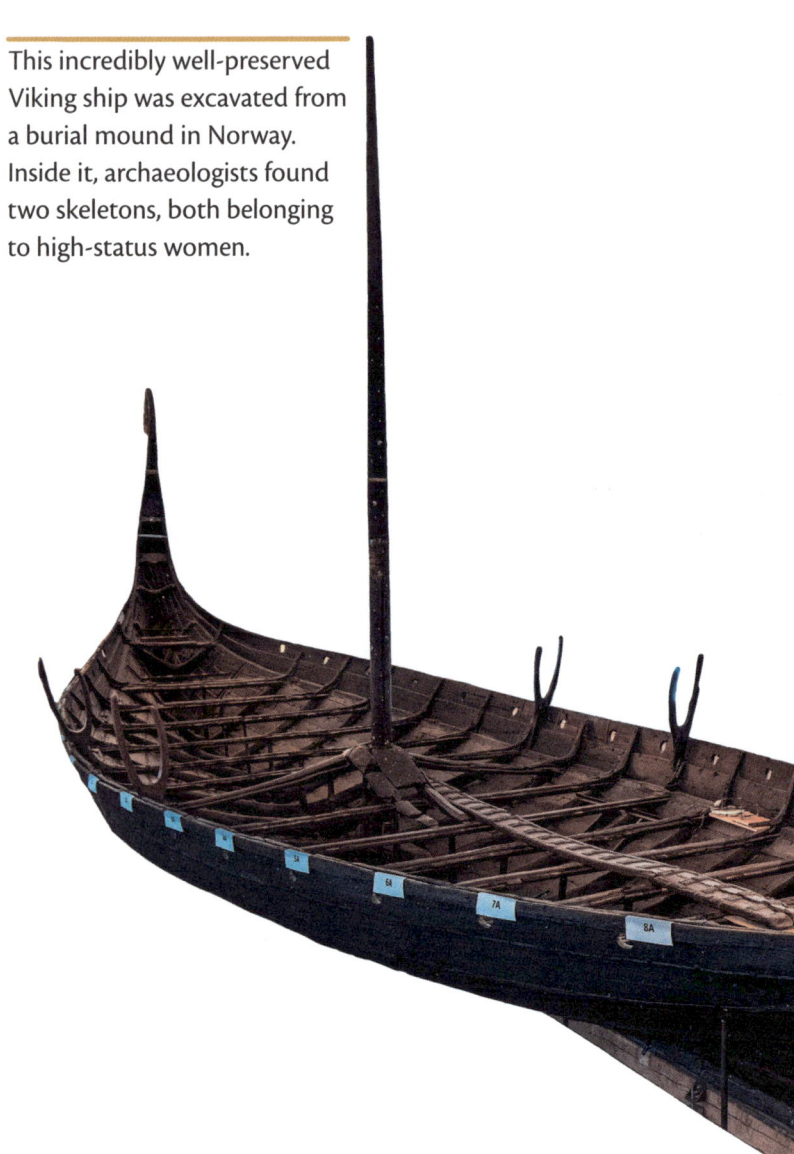

Viking ships varied in size and shape. Some needed to be strong enough to withstand stormy ocean crossings, whereas others needed to snake through narrow river passages. Medieval Scandinavians were expert shipbuilders.

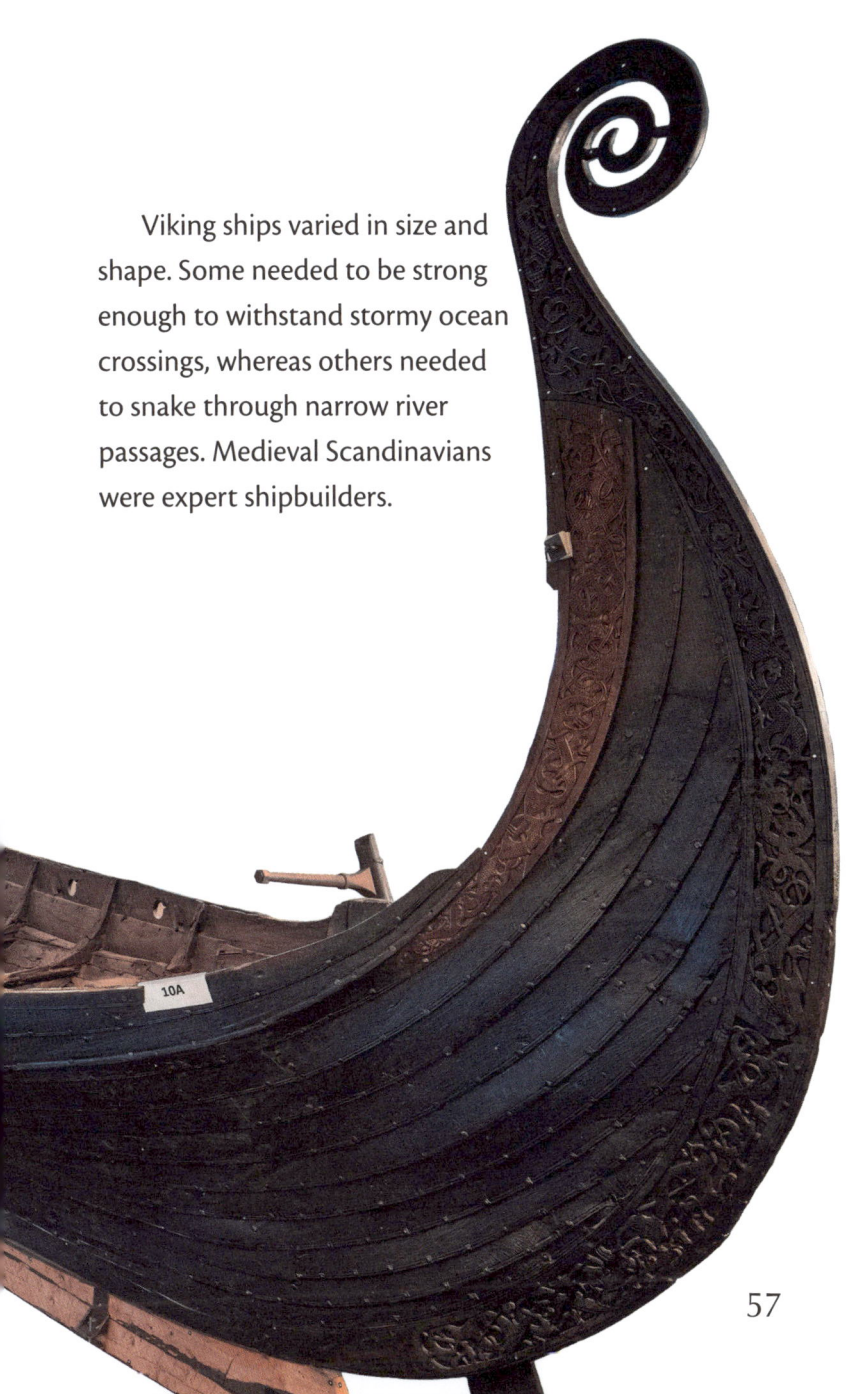

Some Vikings sailed across the North Sea to the coasts of the British Isles, Germany and France.

Around the same time other groups of Vikings set their sights on the Frankish Kingdom (which in time would become France). For nearly 50 years, Vikings raided coastal towns, but in 845 CE, they aimed for a new target: Paris.

This time, the Vikings had an enormous **flotilla** of 120 ships and 5,000 raiders, captained by a raider named Reginheri. The Vikings killed Frankish soldiers and besieged Paris.

Soon though, the Vikings became ill from a plague. Rather than risk being defeated, the Vikings offered to leave Paris if the Frankish ruler, Charles the Bald, would pay them with nearly two and a half tonnes of silver and gold. A deal was struck.

A different kind of Viking Age happened in the North Atlantic, when the first Scandinavian seafarers settled in Iceland. They named it *Snæland*, meaning 'land of snow'. It proved a challenging place to adapt to, even for hardy Scandinavians.

Recent scientific studies show that three quarters of the first male settlers in Iceland were Scandinavian, demonstrating that most of the raiders travelled from what is today Sweden, Norway and Denmark.

But most of the first female settlers appear to have come from the British Isles.

This probably shows that Viking men enslaved large numbers of British women. This seems more likely than hundreds of British women choosing to pair up with Scandinavian raiders all at once.

There is evidence across the Viking world of slave trading, with men taking women and children against their will, and trading them for silver, across all the Vikings' trade routes.

> **FACT**
> Enslaved people were known as *þræll* (thrall) in Old Norse. This is where our word 'enthral' comes from, which means 'captivate'.

Two modern-day countries are named after groups of Vikings. Neither of them are in Scandinavia! Russia and Belarus are named after the Rus, a group of people descended from Swedish Vikings.

The word *Rus* is thought to come from an Old Norse word, meaning 'those who row'. Their route took them not over seas, but down rivers and over land, snaking a trail from the Baltic Sea to the Black sea.

Some Rus then crossed the Black Sea, entering Constantinople, the capital city of the Byzantine Empire. Today, we know this city as Istanbul, the capital city of Turkey.

The Rus Vikings arrived in Constantinople as traders rather than raiders, and they had mostly positive relations with the rulers there. In fact, the very toughest Vikings were invited to serve as the personal bodyguards to Emperor Basil II, the ruler of the Byzantine Empire. These soldiers, known as the Varangian Guard, protected Basil in return for money.

Norse graffiti has been found in the Hagia Sofia, a 1,500-year-old building in Istanbul. At least three runic inscriptions were carved into the marble, saying things like 'Halfdan was here'.

Throughout the time of the Viking raids, one of the most advanced civilisations in the world was the Islamic **caliphate**. In 762 CE, 31 years before Viking raiders first led an attack on the British Isles, a caliph (Islamic ruler) named Al-Mansur founded the city of Baghdad.

Baghdad was the location of the House of Wisdom, the world's largest library. It was a hub where scientists, mathematicians, poets and translators worked together to understand the world. And of course, traders and explorers based in Baghdad travelled widely – including to Constantinople.

Although there is no archaeological evidence proving that individual Scandinavians went to Baghdad itself, medieval Scandinavian and Islamic cultures intertwined in fascinating ways. It was the city of Constantinople itself that formed the main connection between them.

illustration from 1237, showing scholars in Baghdad

Whilst the Rus were in Constantinople, it was the largest and wealthiest city in Europe. It was also at the meeting-point between Europe and Asia. The Rus would have been living alongside Muslim traders, merchants and travellers from Baghdad, soaking up their knowledge, and exchanging goods with them.

Another that connects medieval Scandinavians with the city of Baghdad is silver. Silver was highly treasured by the Vikings, and the value of all things was measured against the weight of silver. Scandinavian traders would exchange their own luxury goods such as honey and animal furs for silver coins called *dirhams*.

For the Vikings, a coin's value was its weight. It would be melted down and reshaped to form jewellery, pendants and armbands. The Vikings learned about accurate measurement from Islamic merchants. They used the weighing techniques being pioneered in Baghdad to ensure they knew exactly how much silver they had, and therefore how wealthy they were.

This silver neck ring was both money and jewellery for its Viking owner.

Most expeditions that the Vikings made were not one-way journeys. Vikings returning to Scandinavia went on to change their home culture, because of their experiences across Europe, Asia and the islands of the Atlantic.

Some Vikings returned home with enslaved people from the lands they visited, some of whom remained as thralls, and some of whom integrated into Scandinavian society. Thralls could sometimes buy their freedom, or they could be freed by those who had enslaved them. Some thralls must have attempted to escape, as laws were written stating how they should be punished.

Most of the places that the Vikings raided had Christianity as their religion. By around 1,000 CE, the powerful rulers in Scandinavia, like Harald Bluetooth, saw great advantages in trading peacefully with their neighbouring Christian kingdoms.

Many medieval Scandinavians adopted Christianity, including the Vikings! This is one of the main reasons the raiding ended. These violent acts went against their new belief system.

Bonus
More about the Birka burial

The warrior grave found in Birka, Sweden, was found to contain a female body.

It was described as "perhaps the most remarkable of all the graves in this field"

It contained a sword, an axe, a fighting knife, two lances, shields and arrows!

Strategy game pieces were placed on the body, suggesting they were a leader.

Experts believe this is evidence of a Viking warrior woman.

 CHAPTER 5

Medieval Scandinavians in Britain

Lots of what we know about the early Vikings comes from British sources. The British Isles were one of the first destinations for Norse seafarers, and it was here that many of their most notorious raids and invasions took place.

Many **chroniclers** and monks created written records about these raids, appalled by the actions of their frightening neighbours from across the North Sea.

Though it was over 1,000 years ago, the legacy of the Vikings can still be seen in Britain today.

The first sign of what was to come was in 789 CE, when traders from Denmark arrived on the south coast of England. When a man called Beaduheard asked them to identify themselves to the king, the Vikings decided instead to kill Beaduheard.

Whilst this was catastrophic for Beaduheard, it wasn't until four years later that the Vikings truly left their destructive mark on Britain.

In 793 CE, the island of Lindisfarne was a quiet place, with a thriving monastery. Monasteries were home to communities of monks, who spent their days praying, worshipping and copying out texts. But the Viking seafarers saw the perfect opportunity to rid this religious building of its valuables.

Lindisfarne was the ideal location for an easy raid – remote, undefended and filled with treasures.

It was a brutal attack. The defenceless monks were murdered or hurled into the sea by the Vikings, and the Viking ships were loaded with stolen goods.

The **sacking** of Lindisfarne outraged Christian Europe. Alcuin of York, a Christian scholar, wrote letters and poetry describing the terrible raid. His writings became a valuable historical source.

Never before has such terror appeared in Britain. Behold the church of St Cuthbert, splattered with the blood of God's priests, robbed of its ornaments.

Raids like this continued occasionally, but around 70 years later, the medieval Scandinavians attempted a full-scale invasion.

The Viking Great Army was formed in 865 CE, with fighters coming mostly from Denmark, Sweden and Norway. Led by two particularly fearless raiders, the brothers Halfdan Ragnarsson and Ivar the Boneless, a fleet of approximately 5,000 raiders arrived off the coast of East Anglia.

King Edmund of East Anglia cleverly offered them horses as a peace offering. The Vikings rested in East Anglia through the winter, before heading north.

The Vikings aimed to take over the most powerful city in Northumbria, which they called Eoforwic (yoff-or-wick). It had been an important Roman settlement called Eboracum. Today, we know this city as York.

Halfdan and Ivar led their army to Eoforwic and quickly gained control. The Kingdom of Northumbria was easy to overpower, as two rival Anglo-Saxon kings were distracted by each other, fighting over who should rule. The Vikings settled their dispute by killing them both.

There's no archaeological evidence of a battle, so it seems likely the threat of Viking violence was enough. The city was renamed *Jorvik* and Halfdan became its first king.

Halfdan Ragnarsson, the first Viking King of Jorvik, 876–877

Jorvik became the centre of the 'Danelaw', which was a large region controlled by the Viking Great Army.

Jorvik became an overwhelming, bustling and **cosmopolitan** city, where goods from foreign lands were traded with merchants and craftspeople. Blacksmiths forged tools and knives, bone-workers carved combs and handles from antler, and weavers and dyers created fashionably-bright cloth.

Cultures from thousands of miles away began to have a subtle impact on life in Jorvik.

Dirham coins from Asia have been found in archaeological excavations of Viking York, showing how quickly goods and people were moving across Europe.

The coin below shows how the two religious cultures in Jorvik, Christianity and Norse paganism, coexisted. On one side of the penny is a cross, and on the other you can see Thor's hammer.

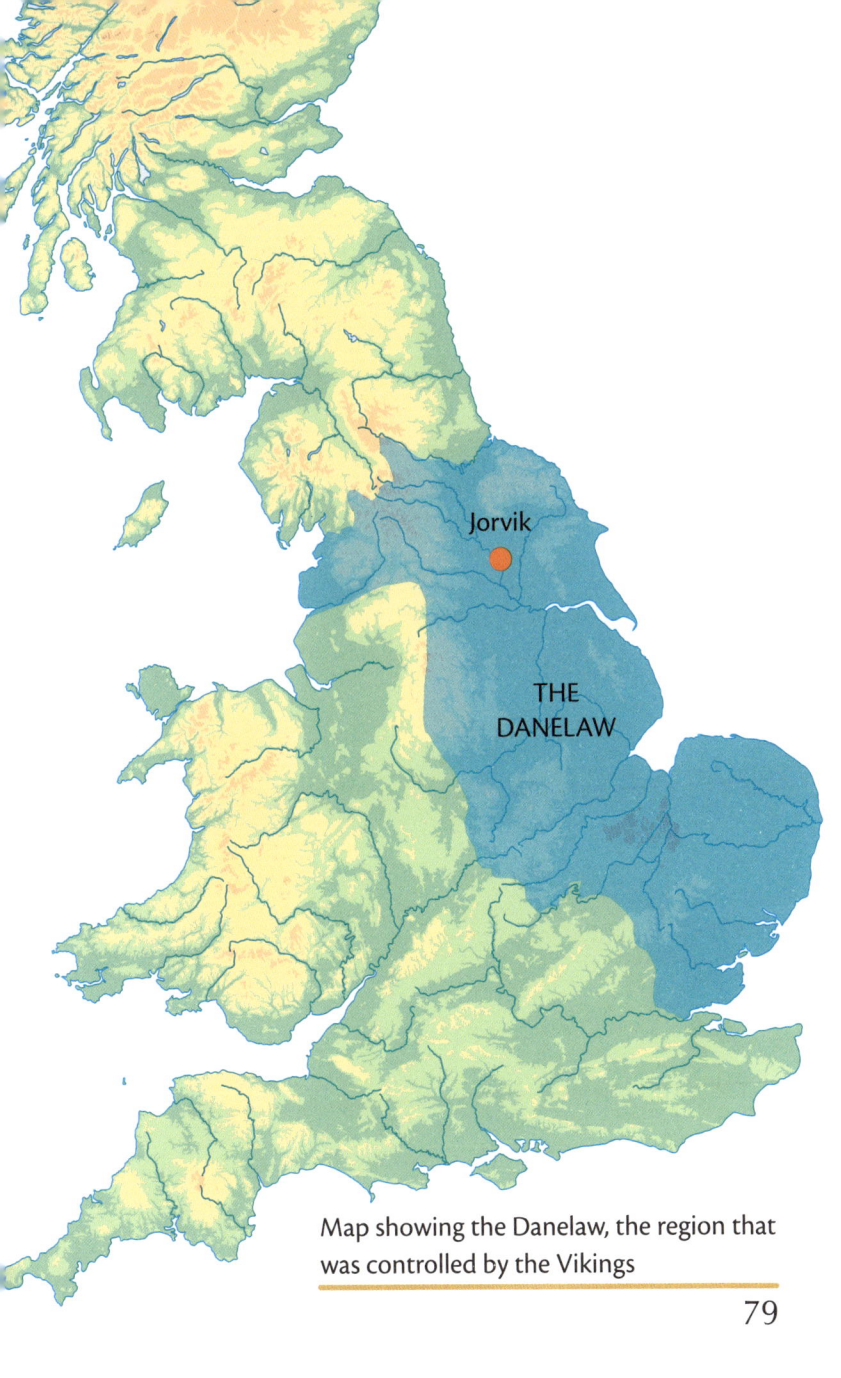

Map showing the Danelaw, the region that was controlled by the Vikings

Viking raids took place beyond the Danelaw too. The islands around Scotland were targets for the raiders, since they could travel to them from Denmark in less than 24 hours. For hundreds of years, the coasts and islands of Scotland faced waves of invasion, raiding and settlement.

Two groups of people, the Picts and the Scots, joined forces to fight back against the Vikings. Their union created the Kingdom of Alba, which can be seen as the beginning of Scotland!

The Vikings had a powerful influence in the British Isles for over 200 years – as raiders, invaders, settlers and even as rulers.

In 1016, a Dane named Canute became King of England. He then also became King of Denmark and Norway.

During this time, Britain wasn't invaded by Vikings because it had become part of medieval Scandinavia.

King Canute, King of England, 1016–1035,
King of Denmark, 1018–1035 and King of Norway 1028–1035.

The Viking Age in Britain came to an abrupt end in 1066. The Kingdom of England was ruled by the Anglo-Saxon Harold Godwinson, but his brother Tostig wanted to be king. Traitorous Tostig schemed with the ruler of Norway, Harald Hardrada, seeking his support.

King Harald Hardrada agreed, and sailed to England, bringing his experienced armies up the Humber estuary towards York. King Harold of England brought his own armies and an enormous battle took place, outside the village of Stamford Bridge.

Harald Hardrada died in battle, and with that, so did the Viking Age in Britain.

the Battle of Stamford Bridge, September 1066

Victory was short-lived for King Harold Godwinson because whilst he was in the North fighting the Vikings, the Normans from France invaded in the South of England. The King of England faced the Norman invaders at the Battle of Hastings, and lost – William the Conqueror became king, and a new period of British history began.

The legacy of the Viking Age in Britain is enormous. Many British places still have Norse names. Settlements ending in -by (village), -toft (house), -beck (stream) and -thorpe (village/farm) all have names that date back to the Danelaw.

Grimsby (Grim's village)

Langtoft (long house)

Holbeck (stream in the hollow)

Cleethorpes (clay villages)

Scunthorpe (Skuma's village)

Today, by looking at a map of England, you can spot the places with a Viking history by searching for names with Norse parts. The study of place names is called toponymy.

Recent scientific research has discovered some remarkable facts. Scientists believe that around 6% of the current UK population have Vikings among their ancestors. That's only a little less than in Sweden, where 10% of the population are believed to have descended from Vikings.

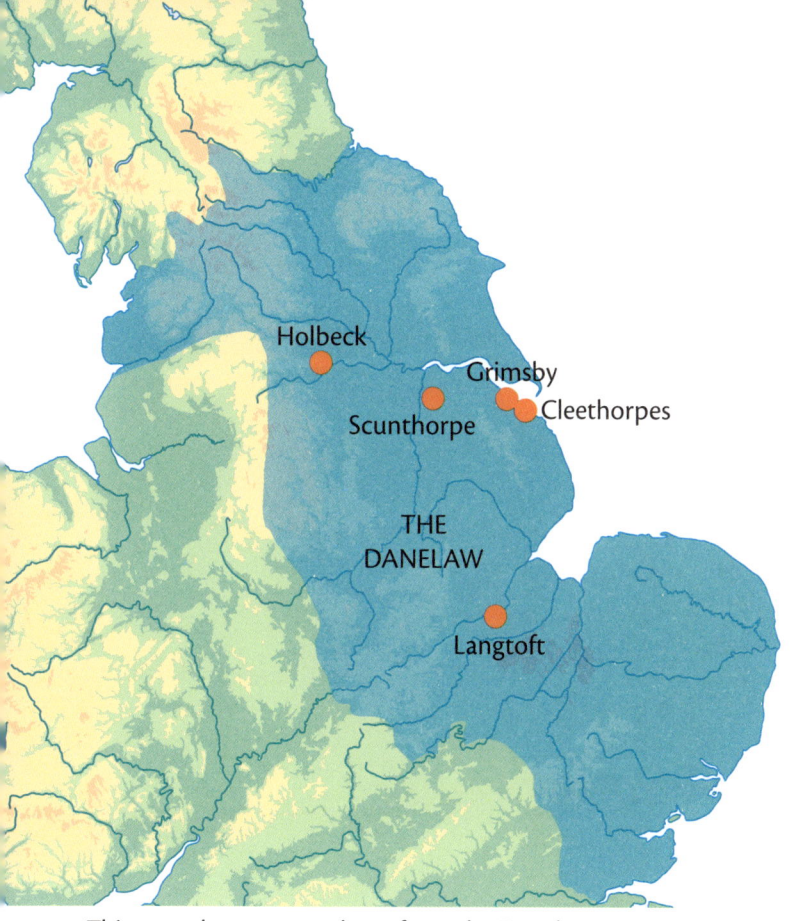

This map shows some places from the Danelaw which still have Norse names.

In the space of a few hundred years, medieval Scandinavian people made a large impression on cultures across the world, and perhaps nowhere more dramatically than in the British Isles.

Norse words in English

The English language still contains lots of words from old Scandinavia.

baggi (meaning a bundle or package) → **bag**

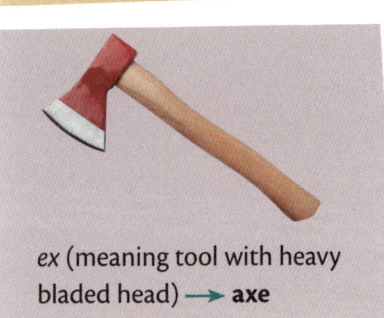

ex (meaning tool with heavy bladed head) → **axe**

egg (meaning unchanged) → **egg**

skith (meaning stick of wood, or 'long snowshoe') → **ski**

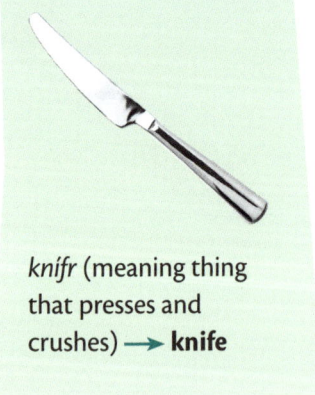

knífr (meaning thing that presses and crushes) → **knife**

vindauga (wind-eye – hole in a wall that air can pass through) → **window**

freknr (meaning scattered things) → **freckles**

ský (meaning cloud) → **sky**

gipt (meaning something given, a present) → **gift**

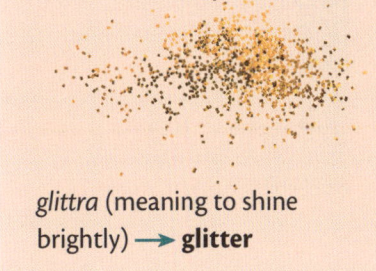

glittra (meaning to shine brightly) → **glitter**

skalli (meaning bald head or skull) → **scalp**

⚛ CHAPTER 6 ⚛
How do we know?

Our understanding of the Vikings and of medieval Scandinavian culture is still developing.

Many experts combine their skills and knowledge to study this period of history, including archaeologists, literature scholars, and experts in the Old Norse language.

Developments in science and technology are revolutionising our understanding, with ever-improving methods to learn more about the artefacts, buildings and bones beneath the ground.

Scientific studies of people's DNA (both living and dead) is yet another way that we are learning what life was actually like in medieval Scandinavia, and in the places that the Vikings visited.

Knowledge does not stay still. When the sources and evidence change, our understanding changes too.

But how do we know what we know?

An archaeologist excavates a burial site in Denmark, 2025.

The written word

Written words tell us a lot. First, writing tells us that at least some people were able to write, using the Futhark runic alphabet. The writing that was left behind – which included carvings on stones, inscriptions on boats and on special objects like pendants and jewellery – tells us what the Vikings valued.

Wherever in the world you find runic writing, that is proof that medieval Scandinavian people traded with that place or travelled to it.

Most longer texts from medieval times were written *about* the Vikings rather than *by* them. The Anglo-Saxons of Britain wrote about them in their chronicles.

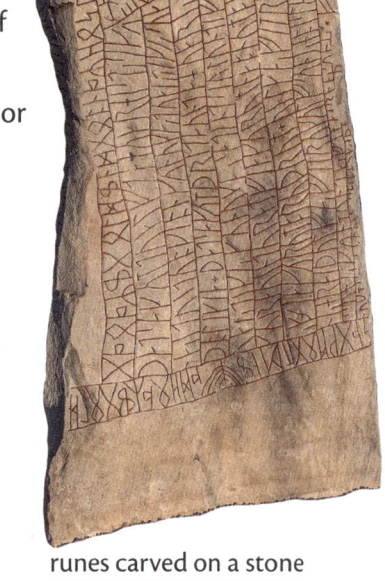

runes carved on a stone

Several Muslim explorers and ambassadors wrote about their encounters with Vikings. Ibn Rustah, a Persian geographer, recorded seeing some unexpected Norse parenting.

'When a son is born, the father will go up to the newborn baby, sword in hand; throwing it down, he says, "I shall not leave you with any property: you have only what you can provide with this weapon."'

Children were expected to become strong-willed and independent.

The famous tales of Norse mythology have only survived until today because they were written down. In the early 1200s, centuries after the Viking Age ended, a historian in Iceland named Snorri Sturluson wrote down the Norse myths.

His text (*Prose Edda*) remains the main source of our understanding of Norse mythology. *Edda* is thought to mean 'poetry' or possibly 'great-grandmother', both of which are great sources of wisdom and stories. It has been translated from Icelandic into many languages.

The *Prose Edda* taught us what medieval Scandinavians believed about their gods and goddesses. This helps us to understand how and why they worshipped them.

Another collection, the *Poetic Edda*, is an anonymous collection of poems about the gods, mostly likely a record of tales passed down by word-of-mouth. The most famous poem is called *Völuspá*, and in it, a prophetess recites the story of how the world was created, and how it will end.

In the *Prose Edda*, Snorri Sturluson described how the goddess Freyja travels about on a cat-drawn chariot.

Artefacts

Archaeologists have unearthed many incredible things from the Viking Age, both big and small.

In York, many Viking hair-combs and board game pieces were discovered in an excavation of the main street of medieval Jorvik. This challenges the view that the Vikings were just violent in the way they were described in the chronicles and journals written by other people.

The 'Vale of York **Hoard**' was an incredible discovery made by two metal detectorists in 2007. They discovered a silver vessel containing 617 coins and 65 other objects, buried in a field.

A gilt silver vessel from the Vale of York

Many hoards of valuables were buried intentionally by people in Viking times, as their prized possessions were safer from theft underground!

Modern archaeology can use the tiniest clue to make some bold discoveries. A particular kind of mouse was only found in Denmark, and in the places that the Danish Vikings travelled to.

Perhaps the mice fancied doing a little bit of raiding themselves?

The bones of a mouse on the island of Madeira were proved to be exactly the same as the 'Norse mouse'. Even though there is no other evidence of a Viking visit to the island, the only explanation for the mouse bones is a Danish ship!

Sometimes, using evidence creates more questions than answers!

Carbon and isotope analysis

More recent scientific developments allow archaeologists to identify the age of things more accurately, especially objects made of living things, like wood and natural cloth. And people too!

All living things absorb tiny amounts of carbon whilst they are alive. When they die, they stop taking it in and the absorbed carbon begins to slowly disappear.

By measuring how much carbon remains in an object, scientists can calculate precisely how old it is.

This method was used to confirm that some Vikings who travelled as far as Greenland actually went further, and spent some time in Newfoundland, Canada.

These explorers cut down trees in Canada to repair their ships, and scientists carbon-dated this wood. The Vikings' metal tools left imprints on the tree stumps, so the scientists confirmed not only that the trees were cut down in 1021, but that Vikings did the chopping.

Viking woodworking tools

Metal tools were not used by the people who lived in Newfoundland before the Vikings, so a Norse visit is the only reasonable explanation.

Isotope analysis is even more interesting. Scientists can study the chemical properties of bones and teeth to work out the details of a person's diet!

Teeth and bones carry special versions of chemicals like strontium, oxygen, carbon and nitrogen. The information they leave on our teeth can be very specific.

Strontium levels can tell us about the specific kinds of soil from which our vegetables were harvested, for example.

This is useful for archaeologists, because teeth are made of enamel, which is even harder and longer lasting than bone, so tooth enamel is often a good source of chemicals to analyse.

If a Swedish woman ate Danish carrots as a child, today's researchers would be able to identify that just from her teeth, 1,200 years later!

In Sigtuna, Sweden, scientists measured the strontium levels of 23 bodies buried between the 10th and 12th centuries. It showed that many of the people were born elsewhere – proving that Sigtuna had a diverse population.

scientists doing an excavation

DNA studies

Our DNA is the code of who we are. Every cell in our body contains our unique DNA code – that's true for the long-dead Vikings too!

Before DNA testing, archaeologists could not usually tell whether human bones belonged to a male or female person, as most male and female bones look identical.

It was DNA analysis that enabled researchers in Birka to discover that the warrior grave they excavated belonged to a woman.

Several archaeologists are revisiting the finds from old burial sites, exploring whether mistakes may have been made when identifying skeletons.

DNA analysis of bones also enables us to discover whether people buried together were related, where in the world they were likely to have come from, and even their physical appearance!

The future of the past

We have a lot more to learn about medieval Scandinavia and the Vikings. One of the most exciting aspects of history is that facts keep on developing.

With every new excavation around the world, with every fortunate metal-detectorist, and with each new development in archaeology, our knowledge of the Viking world continues to deepen.

Let's keep digging for more evidence, and let's start burying the stereotypes.

The factual world of the medieval Scandinavians is far more interesting than the fictional one!

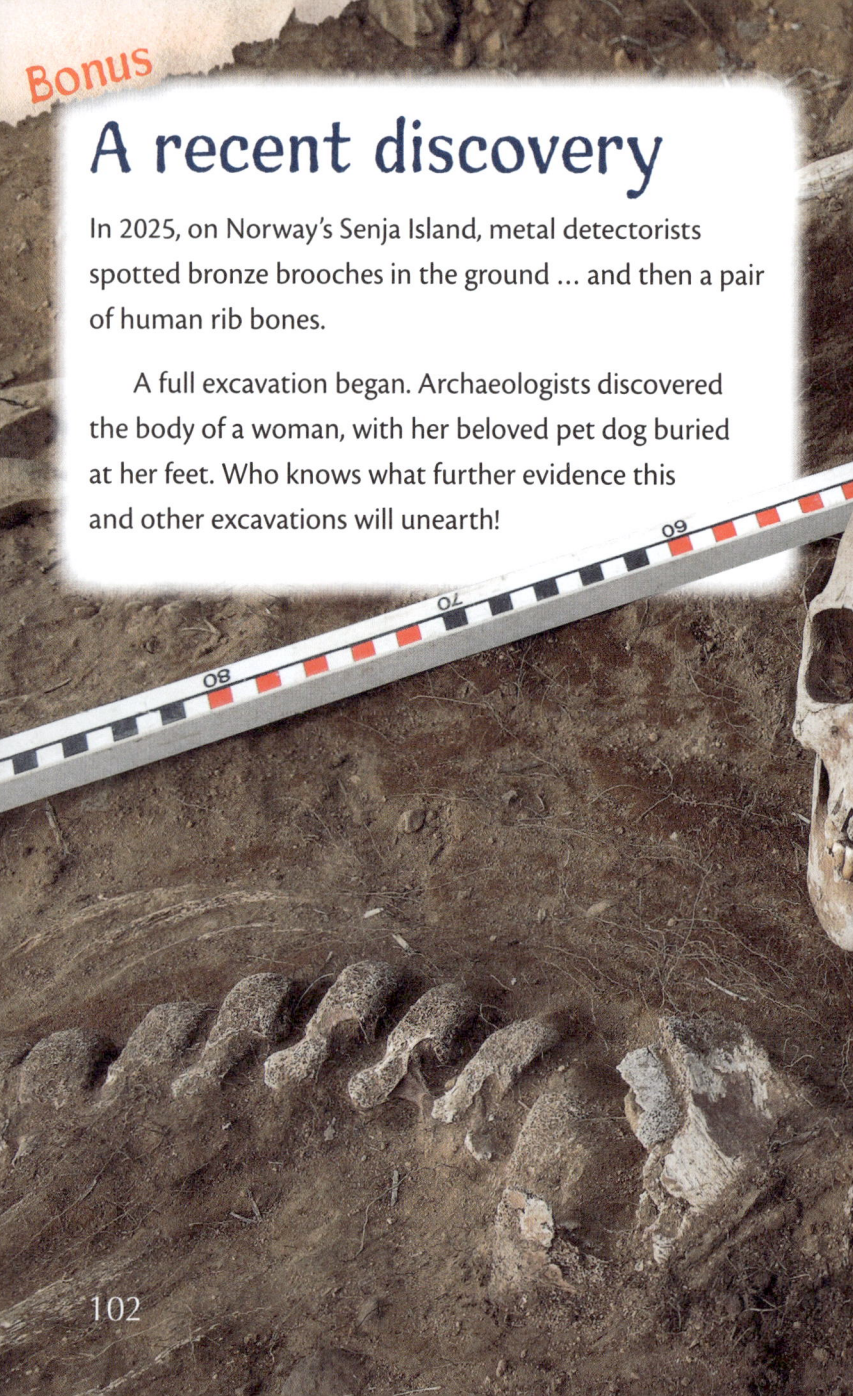

Bonus

A recent discovery

In 2025, on Norway's Senja Island, metal detectorists spotted bronze brooches in the ground ... and then a pair of human rib bones.

A full excavation began. Archaeologists discovered the body of a woman, with her beloved pet dog buried at her feet. Who knows what further evidence this and other excavations will unearth!

Glossary

Anglo-Saxons inhabitants of the British Isles between the 5th century CE and 1066

berserkers Norse warriors who fought with abnormal fury

caliphate the region governed by a Muslim ruler (caliph)

chroniclers people who record events in a book called a chronicle

cosmopolitan a place full of people from many different cultures and countries

flotilla a group of small military ships

hoard a hidden collection of precious things that you have saved

livestock animals raised for humans' use

longhouses the long communal dwellings of medieval Scandinavians

medieval the Middle Ages between ancient and modern times; in European context, between the end of the Roman Empire and around 1500 CE

Norsemen a term used to describe the (mostly) male Viking raiding parties from Scandinavia

raiders people who travelled to attack a place

runes letters from an alphabet formerly used by people in Northern Europe

sacking destroying a place and stealing the valuables from it

sacrifice the act of giving away something valuable, in the hope of gaining good fortune

stereotype a fixed impression that is widely held about a person or thing, often incorrectly and/or unfairly

traders people who buy and sell goods

Valkyries mythical winged women who take dead heroes to Valhalla

About the author

Why did you want to write this book?

I teach mythology and lots of my students love Norse mythology. I thought it would be cool to find out more about the culture these stories came from.

Jonny Walker

Did you know all about the Vikings already or did you research?

I knew a lot about the gods and the myths, but I had to do a lot of research about the new methods in archaeology. I visited old Viking cities like York, went to museums and read lots of interesting books by experts.

What was the most interesting thing you learned while writing this book?

I found out that a village called Nether Poppleton, just outside York in the UK, was not only the site of lots of buried Viking treasures, but it's also where my own ancestors lived in the 1600s!

What do you hope readers will get from the book?

I hope they will feel excited to discover that the truth about the Vikings is actually more interesting than the made-up stories about them. And I hope they enjoy the brilliant illustrations Nuno has created too, which bring the history to life.

Do you think we often get things wrong when we look at history?
Yes! It's important to look at who gets to write about history, and who decides which stories are important enough to share. Working-class people, women and Black and Asian people have often been written about in history books, but haven't had the same chances to research and write their own histories.

Do you think there are more things we still have to discover about the Vikings?
Certainly, yes! Now that archaeologists have so many new methods to study artefacts and human remains, the whole story of who the Vikings were, and what they did, might need to change — and keep changing. That's really exciting.

Do you have a favourite period of history?
I'm really interested in Ancient Greece and the Islamic Golden Age, because both were times of great imagination, invention and writing. I like to learn history by reading what people wrote about at the time.

What would you like to write about next?
I enjoyed learning more about the medieval history of Eastern Europe, whilst I was creating this book. I'd love to research and write about Slavic myths and folklore.

About the illustrator

What made you want to be an illustrator?

I always wanted to do something related to art, animation or illustration. I've been interested in drawing and painting ever since I was a kid. Inspired by animated movies, comic books, and illustrated books, I created my own characters, as well as stories for them, which were always illustrated. Usually there were animals and fantastic places, dragons, knights, forests, castles, wizards...

Nuno Alexandre Vieira

How did you get into illustration?

When I was in college, one of my teachers asked me if I wanted to illustrate an educational book she was writing. That was my introduction to professional illustration jobs – school textbooks. Since then, I've collaborated with several publishers from around the world.

Do you work on a computer or use pens, pencils and paint?

I mainly work digitally, especially on educational books, but I'm always sketching scenes with pen, pencil, and paint, which I then scan. For painting, I generally use the computer.

What was the most challenging thing about illustrating this book?

Perhaps depicting the Vikings clothing and objects accurately, while at the same time maintaining a comical aspect, which was also challenging to keep even in the sad or violent scenes.

What did you like best about illustrating this book?

As I love creating characters, I really enjoyed drawing both the historical and the mythological people, their gods and their monsters, like Fenrir and the serpent Jormungandr. It was also challenging, because there are a lot of versions, which differ greatly from one another, even in terms of hair colour and clothing.

Which was your favourite scene to draw in the book?

I can't pick just one, but it was fun to draw the Vikings when they're leaving Paris, after the pact with Charles the Bald. Also, Freyja in her cat-chariot, and Loki's monstrous sons!

Did you know all about the Vikings, or did you have to do research?

I've always been fascinated by these old civilisations, and particularly the medieval period. The author did a fabulous and meticulous research job, even indicating certain sources, which helped me to see examples of clothing and several other important objects and details. I also did my own research, of course, in order to better portray monsters, gods, and mythological scenes.

Book chat

> **What did you know about Vikings before reading this book?**

> **What surprised you the most while reading?**

> **What was the most interesting thing you learned from this book?**

> **How would you summarise this book in one sentence?**

> **Who would you recommend this book to and why?**

If you could speak to any real person from history mentioned in this book, who would you choose and what would you ask?

If you had to think of a new title for this book, what would you call it?

What do you think is the most interesting real Viking discovery?

Book challenge:

See if you can find any other modern words that originate from **Old Norse**.

Collins BIG CAT

Published by Collins
An imprint of HarperCollins*Publishers*

The News Building	Macken House
1 London Bridge Street	39/40 Mayor Street Upper
London	Dublin 1
SE1 9GF	D01 C9W8
UK	Ireland

© HarperCollins*Publishers* Limited 2025

10 9 8 7 6 5 4 3 2 1

ISBN 978-0-00-879621-1

All rights reserved. No part of this publication may be reproduced, stored in a retrieval system, or transmitted in any form by any means, electronic, mechanical, photocopying, recording or otherwise, without the prior written permission of the Publisher or a licence permitting restricted copying in the United Kingdom issued by the Copyright Licensing Agency Ltd, 5th Floor, Shackleton House, 4 Battle Bridge Lane, London SE1 2HX.

Without limiting the exclusive rights of any author, contributor or the publisher of this publication, any unauthorised use of this publication to train generative artificial intelligence (AI) technologies is expressly prohibited. HarperCollins also exercise their rights under Article 4(3) of the Digital Single Market Directive 2019/790 and expressly reserve this publication from the text and data mining exception.

British Library Cataloguing-in-Publication Data
A catalogue record for this publication is available from the British Library.

Download the teaching notes and word cards to accompany this book at:
http://littlewandle.org.uk/signupfluency/

Get the latest Collins Big Cat news at
collins.co.uk/collinsbigcat

Author: Jonny Walker
Illustrator: Nuno Alexandre Vieira (Beehive Illustration)
Publisher: Laura White
Product managers: Caroline Green and Holly Woolnough
Series editor: Charlotte Raby
Development editor: Catherine Baker
Commissioning editor: Caroline Green
Project manager: Emily Hooton
Copyeditor: Sally Byford
Proofreader: Catherine Dakin
Cover designer: Sarah Finan
Typesetter: 2Hoots Publishing Services Ltd
Production controller: Sophie Waeland

Printed in the UK.

MIX
Paper | Supporting responsible forestry
FSC www.fsc.org **FSC™ C007454**

This book contains FSC™ certified paper and other controlled sources to ensure responsible forest management.

For more information visit: www.harpercollins.co.uk/green

Made with responsibly sourced paper and vegetable ink

Scan to see how we are reducing our environmental impact.

Acknowledgements
The publishers gratefully acknowledge the permission granted to reproduce the copyright material in this book. Every effort has been made to trace copyright holders and to obtain their permission for the use of copyright material. The publishers will gladly receive any information enabling them to rectify any error or omission at the first opportunity.

pp12–13 Eric D ricochet69/Alamy, p14 DNW/Bournemouth News/Shutterstock, pp20–21 Corri Seizinger/Shutterstock, p40 OlgaOzik/Shutterstock, p43 Historic Collection/Alamy, p46 OlgaBegak/Shutterstock, p47 Pecold/Shutterstock, p49 German Vizulis/Shutterstock, p51 The Swedish History Museum/Wikimedia Commons, p52 imageBROKER.com/Alamy, p53t Niels Quist/Alamy, p53b OlgaBegak/Shutterstock, p55 Pobytov/Getty Images, pp56–57 Albert Knapp/Alamy, p60 (background) Naduns_shots/Shutterstock, p64 Heritage Image Partnership Ltd/Alamy, p66 Science History Images/Alamy, p67 Walters Art Museum/Creative Commons, pp70–71 Historic Collection/Alamy, p77 FLHC10/Alamy, p78l Tony Baggett/Alamy, p78r Werner Forman/Getty Images, p81 Chronicle/Alamy, pp82–83 Matthew Paris/Wikipedia, p86tl Katerina Maksymenko/Shutterstock, p86tr Lilkin/Shutterstock, p86c Vinokurov Alexandr/Shutterstock, p86bl Soho A Studio/Shutterstock, p86br VLADIMIR DUDKIN/Shutterstock, p87tl revers/Shutterstock, p87tr Cookie Studio/Shutterstock, p87cl Gergitek/Shutterstock, p87cr houchi/Shutterstock, p87bl Love the wind/Shutterstock, p87br PeopleImages/Shutterstock, p89 James Brooks/Getty Images, p90 Rolf_52/Shutterstock, p93 World History Archive/Alamy, p96 Rob Walls/Alamy, p98 Fnielsen/Wikimedia, pp102–103 Arctic-Images/Getty Images.